Relate!

One Human to Another

TUCKER K. SULLIVAN

Printed in the United States of America
First Printing 2020
First Edition 2020

ISBN: 978-1-7359585-0-7

Disclaimer: The views, thoughts, and opinions in this book are
solely those of Tucker Sullivan. They are weird and possibly
incorrect. Reader advised.

"It's a mutual, joint-stock world in all meridians.

We cannibals must help these Christians"

-Herman Melville, *Moby Dick*

"In this world there's room for everyone,

and the good Earth is rich

and can provide for everyone"

- Charles Chaplin, *The Great Dictator*

Alternately Known As:

Something to Read if You don't like to Read

Moshpits and Libraries

A Few New Clichés

Poems You Could Have Written Yourself

Aphorisms, Anecdotes, and Analogies from an Asshole

Accidentally Plagiarized

A Typo in a Dictionary

Poetry in a Youtube Comment

Geniuses and Saints

Table of Contents

Author's Note

If those of us with opposing views and beliefs made a conscious effort to relate to those we feel most starkly opposed to, we could avoid the bloodshed that is inevitable whenever our belief systems draw lines between us. Given a chance, every human being can relate to any other human being, even if we don't speak the same native language. We all have the same basic needs; food, water, shelter, good sleep, air to breathe, and a place to poop. Politics, religion, race, a favorite sports team, or any other dividing factor we as a species are born with and endure cannot remove these basic needs, which we all share. If we all make an effort to stop arguing (all of us at the same time) and relate to one another, we will find solutions to the issues that have plagued us since the start of our journey, when we first evolved on this planet and began attempting to record our history.

This book is my attempt to relate to the reader, whether you're my friend, my foe, or a stranger. This is a collection of thoughts that have passed through my mind and have come out of that place in the form of a poem or a paragraph. If you do not like the writing, that I understand, but I am sure that there is something else on which we can relate.

Chapter I

42,53,21,22,17,56

Poems about People and Self,

and a couple about

Dreams (Goals),

Dreams (Sleep),

Gratitude, and to Strive

3.18.20.37.**42**.45

Humans should all

  happily relate

    to one another,

       like all dogs

          smell each other's ass.

It's weird but

  IT'S NATURAL.

7.8.18.35.**42**.43.59

We were told we're created

  equal

but it seems

past creation,

    you're on your own.

6.12.**42**

Find friends in

the library,

if there are no readers

stick to the authors.

2.3.4.33.**42**

I miss people

I'll never see

again.

2.6.11.20.26.**42**

Tragedy has been

here on Earth all along,

us humans just

found comedy amongst ourselves.

4.6.8.9.**42**

If we become

   immortal,

I'm meeting all 7 billion of you,

   and everybody

         else.

4.9.33.41.**42**.53

I wonder what my old friends

   would think of me now,

I wonder what my new friends

   would think of me then.

11.40.**42**

The trees are the fur

   and we are the fleas,

some help the host

   some are a disease.

7.**42**.49.62

Car watching

    isn't as good as

people watching.

3.9.16.19.20.**42**.45.62

What if we all had the same last name?

                Tucker Sullivan Human

Hey brother!

    Hey sister!

If names are what and who

                we are,

they should include human.

      One species,

            one family.

1.6.11.29.38.**42**.57

I've never seen anyone else

   here,

but those stacked rocks by the river

  remind me

I'm not the

   only

    one

   who

     likes this place.

18.19.20.**42**.62

A mile is not long enough

to walk in someone's

    shoes.

Why don't you try wearing their

    underwear for like

     a month,

then you can say how well you know them.

    Or just smell it after they wore it for a month.

2.19.33.36.**42**.53

As people we all do wrong,

sadly

    some

       can

          just forget.

8.13.17.18.20.**42**.51

The world has

    no super-powered heroes,

while supervillains are very real.

Still,

    our everyday heroes

        manage to do just as much

            as the ones

               in comic books.

8.18.**42**.47.51

Good people exist.

Good people exist in Islam.

Good people exist in the police force.

Good people exist in the United States.

Good people exist in Christianity.

Good people exist anywhere in this world of ours.

But bad people exist.

So, let's gather these good people.

2.7.13.18.28.**53**

I used to call everything

lame,

terrified I would call something cool

and have someone else call it

the

same,

and that's the lamest thing.

12.31.35.43.**53**

I think when my back story was written

    there were quit a few misspelings and wrong words.

31.43.**53**

I'm the guy

with a decent grasp

    of

       a subject I've been mispronouncing.

2.13.23.**53**.54

Take a stand!

Even though

       there's a comfy bed right there.

7.8.31.**53**.62

I would

    rather be a little much

than not enough.

6.9.37.**53**.62

My mind doesn't really

  wander,

it just goes the wrong way,

  gets lost,

and could use some directions,

  or a GPS,

   or something.

8.18.31.**53**

You told yourself

a thousand times,

when listening

once would do.

36.37.**53**.54

I'm sorry when I'm sitting

right next to you

but I'm far off.

1.6.17.**53**.62

I've stepped on a crack,

      broken a mirror,

walked under a ladder,

      and spilled the salt,

but

  still

was lucky enough,

to find

    a four-leaf clover

 and

    a heads up penny.

What has this got me?

Nothing specific,

    but I'll take it.

8.**21**.44.51.56

No matter

how far

it seems,

reach.

You might be surprised

what you grasp.

22.35.53.54

Damn it.

All this

is way too specific

to be

a

dream.

INTERLUDE ONE

Runes!

Runes, when aligned properly, can shift a person's brainwaves. With a good enough series of runes, you can suspend a person indefinitely. You can conjure up creatures or send people anywhere in the multiverse! With skill, you can confuse or intrigue someone. Best of all, you can use runes to freeze a moment in time. To do this, you assemble a series of runes that aptly portray an event in your life, then whenever you return to that arrangement, you will remember it!

You can also use runes in creative and random ways. For example, if you carve your personal runic title (mine is TUCKER) into a rock, your runic arrangement will remain on that rock for as long as rocks exist, which I think is quite a long time, but I'm not sure; I don't know any earth magic aside from building sandcastles.

21.56.62

Wing it.

    It's the only way to fly.

21.22

Don't go back to sleep

    to chase your dreams

or soon

  you'll be stuck

      in

    a nightmare.

8.**21**.23.37.51.56

Train your brain

    to know exactly

        where

      to go,

when your heart tells it to.

3.4.11.14.**17**.44.58

When rain falls, there's

shelter.

When snow falls, there's

warmth.

When the sun sets, there's

stars.

8.11.**17**.20.37.62

If you want paper

grow a tree.

If you want steak

care for the calf.

Or at least think about it for like 2 seconds,

Jesus, dude.

2.3.6.8.13.23.38.51.**56**

Stranded in the desert,

       trapped in the tundra,

  lost in the jungle,

       abandoned at sea,

or alone in my room,

    I will reach you.

Chapter II

4,14,46,52,41,44

Poems about Time and God,

and a couple about

Heaven/Hell,

the Devil,

Memories, and Faith

4.8.10.31

Infinity

    allows it.

Eternity

      ensures it.

4.8.20.35.62

Time is our

      only

       resource.

4.6.10.14.18.37.43

There is a guy

 in charge

   of

sorting all the parallel

        universes,

his name is Time.

4.10.18.29.51

There

    is

no such thing

      as done.

While the sun will one day

      stop burning,

ours is not the only one.

4.9.11.17.20.29

    Sit

just long enough

    to see

the light change.

4.23.35

Time will take

     us there,

in a hurry

     and oh so slow.

4.14.31.35.43.53.61

Time told me

     everything I know

and even spaced it out

     so my brain

          didn't explode.

4

Something that

     lasted

a tenth of a second

     exists forever.

4.8.10.15.29

No matter how big space

                looms

it's just a speck of time.

4.10.11

Plenty of time to watch the

                        sun rise,

and plenty left to watch

                        it set.

4.10.29.35.58.61

The paint is time

  when it dries

the masterpiece is

        life.

2.**4**.31.36.37.42.43.62

We're all murderers for

        killing time.

4

It's never finished,

      but it's always done,

           you can rush to

              greet it,

    or you can watch it come.

4

Time was here

long

    ago

and it will be here

    even

      longer

    from now.

4.10.31.62

Then

    now

        when,

again

    and again

        and again.

4.8.10.15.20.35.42.47

It's impossible to see

    eternity,

so humans were made

 to see

    one second

        at a time.

1.2.**4**.17.20.35.51

You have

the time

    of a life.

4.35.53

All we get

  in

    life

  is

    time,

we better learn

  to

    use it

      wise.

4.14

Past   Future

            Present

        trinity of Time

4.10

Without time,

        space

would still

        be tiny.

4.10.**14**.15

I think God

    is

a struggling artist

        who was given eternity

            for a deadline.

2.**14**.19.51

 God does not

cause suffering,

He survives it

        with us.

8.**14**.16.23.42.49

God is up there like,

"Who told them about ribosomes

and mitochondria?!

They know it's the powerhouse of the cell?!

Getting pretty damn smart,

I'm proud."

8.10.**14**.20.31.49

We imagine super-human powers

but then

there are God's powers,

don't confuse the two.

We'd all be invincible

if

God lets us be

for long.

7.13.**14**.20.27.31

When they say, God

you hear "ruler"

when you say, God

they hear "creator"

when I say, God

I mean "everything."

Then we argue over God's existence,

ignorant of what the other person even meant.

2.3.10.**14**.53

We constantly fight with God

while

forever cradled in his arms.

2.6.**14**.47

If you need a hand to hold onto,

you can always pray.

2.**14**.17.18.20.59.62

You can thank God

       for seeing you through,

or curse him for

       putting you through,

the event

       remains the same.

2.**14**.16.56

And when he met

       God

He asked,

       "that all you got?"

INTERLUDE TWO
If We Kill

If you kill my son

I will kill your brother,

and if I kill your brother

you will kill my father,

and if you kill my father

I will kill your daughter,

and if we both keep killing,

We will

kill each other.

So, if you choose to

love me

and I choose to love you,

We will meet each other's

families

and we will know what's

better.

10.13.**14**.15.19.62

Imagine the sun is your religion

      it gives life, light, vitamin D, and electricity,

but if you're not careful, it can burn you.

      Religion shouldn't burn anyone.

We should only use it for light,

          life,

            love, and vitamin D.

14.52

The devil said,

"you may have made all the rules, but I'm not afraid to break them to win."

God replied,

"it has never been a game."

8.13.44.46.51.**52**

The devil's advocate

secretly works for

      Angels

preparing them to fight

      the devil,

no matter what he says.

2.4.18.38.**46**.62

When you're headed

      to hell,

it's best to take your

      time.

2.**46**.49.53.62

I can stand the heat,

      just hope hell ain't humid.

18.34.**46**.62

Don't speak ill of the dead,

you don't want it awkward

      in hell.

4.20.35.**41**.62

This moment

    is

memory

    already.

1.4.8.**41**

All those things you look forward

          to,

make damn good memories.

15.**41**.43.53

I don't really

       want a

photographic memory.

The

   paintings

       have been fine.

4.26.**41**.62

If looking

   back

doesn't make you laugh,

you might not

     have done enough

       dumb shit.

10.14.15.31.40.43.**44**.48.53.62

I believe in

      everything,

and each of its

        meanings.

.

Chapter III
11,57,40,38,6

Poems about Nature and Exploration

And a couple about the World,

Travel, and Seeking

4.8.**11**.29.50.51

A beautiful

    wildflower

is food for

    a deer

 and

    turns to shit,

but the antlers grow.

2.**11**.13.18.20.34.35.50

For every animal

    devoured,

another has a nice meal.

2.6.8.**11**.20.23.44.50.51.56.57

 If all you see is

    mud

   press on,

water must be near.

10.**11**.13.14.28.30.40.42.47.50.51

Earth

  doesn't seem to have

sufficient

  white blood cells

    to eradicate

      us humans.

Hopefully no outside

      prescription medication

comes down

      from the sky.

We should probably

     attempt to

live to reach a more symbiotic

      relationship

with our

   host.

9.**11**.15.16.20

Crabs

    think

  we walk sideways,

      and

giraffes wonder

    how we look around,

and eat the

      leaves off trees.

6.8.9.**11**.20.23.29.56.57

Climb to the top

   of a mountain.

You'll see way more than

   whatever

      was

        at

    the bottom.

6.7.**11**.20.38

I saw a man

    on the path

across the river

      while I bushwhacked,

we waved

  and walked

     opposite directions.

6.8.**11**.13.23.38.56

Sometimes you must ford

     the river

    to follow it.

1.**11**.29.53.58.61

As I stare up at this tree

    I'm less alone

     though

       It's still just me.

6.8.**11**.17.20.49

The eagle watched

the cheetah from the sky

        wishing it could run.

(shut up about eagles not living

where cheetahs live or whatever,

you get what I'm going for here)

11.42.53

I think if a river

      was a person

we would be

      the best of friends.

We would rush to adventures,

      then hang around lazily,

probably drunkenly pour our hearts out.

Man,

      me and that river go way back.

8.**11**.23.29.31.58

From the mouth

    of the river,

spoke a steady

       stream.

4.6.**11**.17

If you can find the times to look

       for four-leaf clovers,

you find yourself lucky already.

11.17.29.35.61

No matter how dense

    a forest's leaves,

    the rain

will reach the roots

    to feed,

  become more and more

      dense and green.

2.3.4.8.**11**.35.44.51

A blade of grass

   might get tread on

but don't worry

     the field always comes back,

even after the harshest

         winters.

6.8.**11**.23.29.51.53.56.57

Charge through the brambles

     the thorns scratch, and bleed

shoes covered in mud

    head swarmed by flies

but keep going

   reach what's beyond.

A river, a meadow, the ocean,

      a mountain

        walk on

          and on

        and on.

11.13.23.50.58

Rock to rock

    to rock, shit!

      My foots in the water.

That's what you get when

         you dance with a river.

11.58

Rain rain,

    come again

let the flowers

    drink it in.

7.8.**11**.50

One

    rock

      can change

the

    current.

1.9.**11**.29.38.57.62

The beach is a

       weird place.

There're birds

       that'll steal your food,

and children become kings and queens

             of sand,

and I SWEAR I just saw a guy standing up on wave out there.

11.13.20.29

A bird has the balls

    to hug its wings

      and dive

because it knows

    all it needs

      to do

is unfurl them

    to fly.

4.**11**.34

Years of autumns ago
      this log
took "fall" too literally.

6.9.**11**.16.18.47.57

How close can I get
      to the river
 and still stay dry?
I will go until I fall in,
      then
        I'll
          close to know.

11.44

I can appreciate an atheist's faith
           in nature.

1.**11**.17.20.29

The shade under a tree

      is a sweet place to be.

You get some shade,

      while the tree gets some light

and a little bit of company.

2.4.**11**.33.34.62

They cleared the trees

      here

  a while back,

then they put some solar panels.

I guess that's

better than pavement,

but the trees are

      still gone.

6.8.9.11.23.38.51.56.**57**

True exploration

  will

reveal much

   that is mundane

     and then

      suddenly

     the unbelievable.

So, if you're bored,

     off exploring,

  be excited!

8.9.23.38.56.**57**.58

Walking

    nowhere

always brings you

      somewhere,

and dead ends don't bother you

        at all.

INTERLUDE THREE

Hope

I hope I never have to
use a fire extinguisher

and I hope you
never need stitches.

I hope you never
need antibiotics

and I hope
I never need to use a firearm.

The thing is,
   we will have to deal with worse

but I hope not anyway.

And fuck a totaled car.

11.20.61

I hear the chirping flock of

      chickadees,

but all I see are leaves.

I wish that I could see

      the city in the tree.

4.**11**.28.35.58.62

    Scientists say

we evolved from apes,

but further and further

   back,

      we come from phytoplankton

and trees.

Our great-great-great ones

    still give

     us air to breathe.

6.8.9.11.56.**57**.58

If you haven't been caught off guard

in your wandering

wander a little further.

If and when you come across something crazy

sit down

right

where you are.

Then rise

and wander more.

1.6.11.20.29.42.**57**

Find a spot that you can sit and stare

and never know

a human's been there.

6.8.9.10.20.38.**40**.56.57.58

The rest of the

world

is right outside the

door.

16.20.**40**

Could you be a patriot

for the

whole

world?

9.10.20.**40**

A man of numbers knows that

the world does

not add up.

A man of words knows that

the world can't

be defined.

8.18.23.**40**.42.47.51.62

We need

    one or two

more geniuses

    added to the population,

to make the whole world

        more smarter.

6.8.10.11.21.**38**.51.56.57

An astronaut

    to

      Titan

   packed

  a pair

   of

    skis.

6.35.**38**.56.58

The way has become

overgrown,

but I remember it leads

straight home.

6.8.23.35.**38**.51.56

It's a long way off

but I'm going anyway.

It's a long way off

but I'm on my way.

It was a long way off

but I'm finally close.

Now, it's a long way back.

2.8.13.35.**38**.39.51.58

Pack away

    a little

        peace,

bring it everywhere

      you go.

6.8.13.23.**38**.53.62

I've come

      quite a way

   now,

I hope it's the right direction.

    I don't want to

      have to

        turn

          around.

Chapter IV
60,23,13,28,27,24

Poems about Government (fuck) and Progress

and a couple about Danger,

Opinion,

Disagreement,

and Money

8.13.18.23.27.40.42.47.51.56.**60**

It's clear we've been

divided

let's hope we are not

conquered.

It's still completely possible

to unite

and

thrive.

18.20.27.28.42.**60**.62

Republicans and Democrats

both

hate that pothole.

6.7.8.15.16.20.27.28.31.37.42.47.49.51.59.**60**

We've established

    left

       right and center.

They kinda suck,

Can we

    all try to be above?

20.31.34.40.58.**60**

Kings used to

    lead the charge.

Now politicians

    sit behind a desk,

and choose who starves.

18.31.42.43.**60**

Nobody

    is the majority,

so, no one wins and everyone's mad.

18.19.20.23.27.42.47.**60**

They clearly want us

    arguing.

Does anyone want to hang out

    and see what we

        agree on?

27.28.59.**60**

Democrats hate

    Wall Street

Republicans hate

    Washington

and then they fight each other

    instead of

        fixing either thing.

13.20.27.53.**60**

Those on the edges

      scream

at us in the middle

"come right!"

      "come left!"

and we go either way we're facing.

But if we look around,

      we notice

they are on the edges,

      about to fall off.

20.28.**60**.62

I like how they say "voting for"

      instead of "rooting for"

        as if

it's not some big game.

13.20.27.28.49.59.**60**

Politics is like two

    cults in an argument.

If Scientologists were in a

    fight with

Westborough baptists

YOU WOULDN'T TAKE A SIDE

    Right?

    You would laugh,

        Right?

    Please laugh.

2.7.12.13.27.51.61.**60**

He brought the books

    they told him to burn,

    but

He ripped out his favorite pages

        first.

2.13.16.24.27.28.34.40.**60**

What is the difference

between a man killing another man

who stole from him,

and a country waging war against a country

over economic policy?

not

just numbers.

13.31.34.40.**60**

Everyone knows

the pen is mightier than the sword,

but what about the keyboard?

It's a modern thing,

to destroy a small country right from

your

office.

9.11.13.16.40.**60**

Is there anymore land

      not owned by man?

Acres and acres

      just bought and sold.

Labeled forever

      by people I don't know.

31.42.43.49.**60**.62

If cops are

      pigs

and people are

      sheep,

the oligarchy is a damn good farmer.

8.23.56.**60**.62

The unity

    created to fight

       the dystopia

could be the start

     of the utopia.

If you believe

    in those sorts of

        things.

27.**60**.62

One side wants to ban guns

    the other

      crack down on immigration,

both forgetting without

       either

    we wouldn't have a nation.

31.49.**60**

It's more of an "eh-lection"

  because half the country says

"eh" and doesn't even vote

hahaa,

    Right?

     Anyone?

       Anyone?

2.3.4.18.19.20.**23**.34.35.36.41.62

My ancestors

     probably killed

my best friend's

     ancestors.

It is sad,

    but we're best friends now.

1.2.17.20.**23**.35.53

Hiding in the bathroom

    because I hate this class.

     Hiding in the bathroom

       from Dad.

Hiding in the bathroom

   to smoke my reefer.

Hiding in the bathroom

     because this party sucks.

Now I'm just shaving.

    Feels nice.

4.8.**23**.56

Do until it's done,

then go do something new.

4.6.8.13.16.**23**.56

In life

    every second

        is

    closer to the end

than it is

    to the

        beginning,

so, what the fuck

    have you been doing?

6.7.8.**23**.38.57

Be sure to

make a plan,

but don't worry

    how

according

    it goes.

8.13.**23**.35

If you keep paying attention

      to things people say

        behind your back,

you'll always be turning around

      and you'll never move forward,

and if you keep saying things

        about people

         behind their backs,

someone's going to hear you

     and punch you in the mouth.

13.18.20

Talk all the shit you want,

     just realize

there's poop in your mouth.

8.18.**24**

I would rather be lucky

           than

             rich.

24.62

We shuffle

  dollar bills and

    pennies around

pocket to pocket

  but the ones

 calculating

    and keeping track

could care

    less

  about

a dollar

   or a

     cent.

20.**28**.43.59

I think

   we might divvy up

      these atoms incorrectly.

11.**13**.20

There was a bird

 who lost his flock

  and missed the hunter's guns

there was a fish

 who lost his school

  and just slipped past the nets.

Be careful who

    you roll

      with.

INTERLUDE FOUR
Humanity's Problem

Our only problem as a species is our long-term survival. One day the sun will explode; this is a scientific fact. Most of us seem to shrug and say, "we will be long gone by then." Okay, true. Then where will we be?

Our only solution to this problem is to advance our knowledge far enough to travel far away from this blessed, destined to explode, sun of ours.

11.**13**.20

Humans were once

   superstition to animals.

"They make pure light and heat

          at night"

"They have more calls than any bird"

"They can even put plants

     in rows wherever they want"

Now animals know better.

1.6.8.**24**.62

My dream job is getting paid

    for all this shit

       I'm already doing.

1.18.**24**.25.53.62

Found eighty bucks on the ground,

    gave it to who I thought

          maybe

        had dropped it,

it's their lucky day,

and I'm a dummy.

11.**13**.18

It's not our thumbs

    that made us great,

raccoons and monkeys

    have thumbs.

It's that we learned

    to burn things,

and if we're not as smart

    as we pretend to be

we'll burn our whole world down.

10.20.**27**.42

It's like we're arguing over

the names of constellations,

      while

knowing nothing of the stars.

28

I fucking

    hate

      opinions.

Chapter V

31,12,55,25

Poems about Words/Language and Reading/Writing

And a couple about

Media/TV/Movies,

and Music

18.**31**.36

Would've

   is as good as

didn't.

13.18.27.**31**.47

Words

   will always be more effective than

bullets.

We can talk

   while the guns are

pointed.

12.18.**31**

Nothing is just written,

   it is either

      said

      or it is

         read.

31.43.62

Oblivious

  and obvious

    are spelled way too close.

13.18.20.**31**.42

It is possible

    to be

eloquent,

  articulate,

   and

completely wrong.

10.11.12.15.**31**

We imitate with letters

    and numbers

  what the universe first did

    with

     atoms.

1.6.8.9.12.29.**31**.58.62

"Something came out of it"

   is an amazing phrase.

Because it's never like, I got my suitcase

    and something came out of it

or

  something boring like that.

It's always,

   we couldn't find his house

     so we drove around

       but we ran out of gas

     so we walked through the woods

and I got poison ivy

     but we saw a cool waterfall

so something came out of it,

and that's

   just great.

6.12.16.**31**.35.49

We all want the meaning of life

   so,

      Webster's dictionary defines it as…

Actually, no wait

   I think I would rather

  have some synonyms for life,

what is life like?

   Grab a thesaurus.

2.3.**31**.35

So fascinating and simple,

  the little

phrases we come across in our lives

  that change everything.

  "Will you go to dinner with me?"

"I've had enough of your shit"

  "I love you"

"Not guilty"

8.12.**31**.37.58.61

Ups, downs,

  roundabouts,

     out of bounds

and weird sounds,

then randomly

     when you take a verb and noun

a thought pops out.

12.**31**.62

Funner is a word

   because it's more fun

to talk that way.

31.53.62

Boredom is

   what boredom

doesn't.

15.**31**.37.50

Certain sounds

    pronounced,

bounce

    in the brain

and magically,

    images appear.

11.12.18.**31**.43.49.53.62

I know this is some corny shit,

      but corn

    is one of the most versatile

        plants on the planet

and I may be sappy,

  but sap

    makes maple syrup

the best condiment on the planet.

1.3.**31**.39

I wish there were

      a word

for when you feel

    what you're alive for

there might be some word,

     a more learned man would know

  but it's such a specific feeling

    when

the surfer enters the water

    when the composer hears the sound

when the painter sees the color

  I wish there

were a word

oh well,

    just go feel it.

1.12.26.**31**

If every sentence were poetry,

    and conversation verse,

      laughter

  would be the best punctuation.

12.13.15.**31**.43.62

Stories purposely made to not make any sense

              suck.

My horse was sick

    so I took it to the shop,

  so my son couldn't make it on the right day,

      but he was happy about the color,

so I'm not sure what to do.

No shit, that didn't make any sense.

    It's interesting and odd

      language allows it

    at all.

31.62

I love when the word romantic

    is used

        to describe

something unrelated to a relationship or love.

10.**31**.43

  This wouldn't be

    without

that, those, and these.

12.28.**31**.37.53.62

My favorite phrase is

    "I could be wrong"

because

    it allows me

to say whatever the fuck I want

with very few consequences,

    but I could be wrong.

8.12.15.**31**.37.40.47.51

The dictionary may

       have every word

yet it's no work of art,

but

   two percent of those words

put

  together

      can completely change the world.

12.15.16.**31**

When did we stop

      creating new words?

Is anyone allowed to,

      or do you have to be a linguist,

or a Ph.D. or a Liberal?

  Let's start again,

<u>Cratawerd</u> – (v., n.) v, to create a new word. n, a
movement to create new words.

     I'm sure that one will stick.

12.**31**.62

I like words

    that give thesauruses

trouble.

9.18.**31**

There is an ancient language

    friend, amigo

      aloha, hello

give the brain some

    sound waves

    somehow it knows.

12.15.**31**.37

Black and white

    across a page

colors and visions

    in the brain.

9.14.**31**.62

There is a big difference between

      the powers that be

and

      the higher power.

6.8.**12**.23.53.56

Read three pages of a

self-help book

and

    love

every word.

2.3.**12**.31.33.37.39

You think you

     got to me

but I didn't write a word

      about you

Oh, fuck, wait.

12.14.15.46.49

All the writers

      and the physicists

   go to hell

      God doesn't need that kind of

            competition.

4.**12**.20.31.37

It takes less than a second

      to read a sentence,

that says a year has passed.

12.31.49.53.57

If I came across a book of my life

　　　that appeared to contain the future

I wouldn't read the end.

I would definitely check to see

　　　if there's a glossary

　or appendix,

Maybe a cool map in the front?

INTERLUDE FIVE

Ignorance Is Agony

Ignorance is a lack of knowledge, to be unaware. Society tends to suffer from ignorance, whether it is ignorance of its government's actions or ignorance of the tragedies happening right there in the societies themselves. Yet sadly, people argue that "ignorance is bliss" and "what you don't know won't hurt you." That philosophy is the wrong one. That philosophy is the equivalent of attempting to ignore an infection until it heals because it is gross and ugly to look at. Still, society remains ignorant. Even if a people within a country were fully conscious of every action its government took, it would be ignorant to the rest of the world. Knowledge of something makes you care about that something, caring is the first step to helping. Ignorance is agony, knowledge is bliss.

12.16.39.43.53

Do you ever read

    a specific reaction someone

had or a face someone made

      in a book

so you try it out

    a few times yourself

to make sure you have the image, right?

12.15.31

Tropes

  must have been genius before.

12.31.59.62

  In the name

of the author,

    reader,

and holy words.

    Amen.

12.31.42

A good library

   is a fulcrum

in the universe

      of perspectives

of authors

and characters

   and historians

and other dimensions,

  our dimension

      in particular.

12.50.62

I use gel pens

   because they told me

not to in school.

12.31.43.62

Prosetry and stanzagraphs

English teachers HATE them.

3.4.10.29.42.**55**

Juliet has nothing

     on

Topanga

  Pam Beesly

  and

 Juno,

Lindsay Weir

  and

Wendy Peffercorn.

and Princess Leia

    and Hermione,

and all the badass women of

    the multiverse.

1.7.20.**25**

Some snap their fingers

    to the drums,

some hum with

  the base,

some wail

  with the guitar,

and the lyrics

 hit us

  each

with deep and different

  meaning.

We all love the song.

20.42.**55**

We need cops like

  Jim Hopper

    not

  John Rayburn.

1.**25**.37.58

There's a song in my head

    I do not know the tune.

There's a song in my head

    I don't know the lyrics to.

There's a song in my head

    I just hum along.

There's a song in my head

    I'll try to pass it on.

7.18.21.26.43.**55**.58

Keep it high and tight,

    follow proto,

        try it out,

        don't be stingy.

    We need a rational revolution,

the cool guy club is waiting.

Chapter VI
16,58

Poems that are Questions

And Poetry-ass Poetry

11.**16**.18.49

Is the ultimate

level of Buddhism

   when you're just

     totally

      chill

   with bugs crawling everywhere?

16.35.43

Is life a magic trick?

   A science experiment?

A math problem?

   A colossal coincidence?

I'm no authority,

   but to me, it's all and more,

      and more and all.

16.20.35.37.41

Does everything we perceive

    stay somehow,

        physically,

in our brain's raw memory?

What is the universe keeping?

    Or is

this just a human way of thinking?

9.11.13.**16**.23.50.59

Is evolution an unstoppable progression

      or can we

      devolve?

If it is possible

    to devolve,

has it happened

      to any species already?

How can we make sure it doesn't happen to us?

I need a biologist.

13.**16**.42.44.53

Am I crazy

    for placing faith

in humanity?

9.**16**.37.53

Can someone help me?

I seem

    to be existing,

and I don't know

        how to stop,

or start again,

actually.

8.**16**.31.43.58

If you're a being

    but you stop doing

are you?

11.**16**.40.47.62

What if collectively

    we stopped

walking past litter

    thinking

      "That's not mine"?

9.10.11.**16**.20.31.58

We are as small

  as a cell,

when we stand

  next to a star.

So what is an atom

To this Sun of ours?

16.18.20

If I steal your water,

do you want my piss?

We only need some

    things to live.

15.**16**.18.37

If something

    imaginary

        makes you catch your breath

isn't it

    a little bit real?

13.**16**.17.32.42.51

Can I ask

    you

something personal?

16.35

When I open my eyes
  should I be
    surprised to find
      life?
Or is all this more
    common than it seems?

9.10.**16**.18.62

Google can't answer
    the real questions,

Is the moon really made of
  cheese?
What should I have for breakfast?
    Why do we exist?

11.**16**

Does a

    tree

        feel

    the forest?

8.9.10.14.15.**16**

The greatest

        invention

        was the imagination,

who thought

        of such a thing?

1.3.**16**.56

If you're not doing

      what you love,

what are you doing?

2.**16**

How dark

    can it get?

I know bright

      light burns

but,

    how dark

        can it get?

9.13.**16**.17.35.47.62

How many

      lives

has that stop sign saved?

4.13.**16**.20

How long does it take

    for a ship

floating

      without a sailor,

to sink

   beneath the sea?

20.31.35.**58**

Bad luck

  turns to

    must

3.**58**

It seems

  it's

    mostly

      about love.

27.28.40.43.**58**.62

The world is

 having

  arguments

and all the sides are

                    bad

because, if you think about it, the world

      can't really be

            divided equally

   it's a weird sphere

and there's

    oceans

and all the countries

   borders are

      squiggly....

just doesn't work.

INTERLUDE SIX

Dangerous Worldview

A 99 to 1 worldview,

the world is

99% good

1% bad,

for every negative thing

there are 99 positive things,

this is dangerous

because the evil 1%

cannot have us

know

how close they are to losing.

BUT

if I'm an idiot,

and that ratio is backward

and it's 1 good to 99 bad,

that doesn't really change

the fact

we live for good.

1.9.10.11.17.20.29.42.43.**58**.61

On the land

  and undersea

under stars

  and all we see

everything is you and me

impermanent,

completely free

everything is

     us and

     we.

2.9.11.13.29.39.40.**58**.61

Spanish moss,

  an albatross

or whatever

kind of bird.

It's an awesome world

  we choose to burn.

4.9.10.11.16.34.35.53.**58**.61

Cosmic conundrums,

like where'd we all come

from?

Does time tick the same

for humans and

fish?

And when I die

what exactly comes

next?

I'll think til I die

that's freedom,

I guess.

6.7.8.31.38.53.56.57.**58**

I ran away

from everything

at walking pace

I guess I strolled away.

9.13.18.**58**.62

I was afraid of the dark

    because

it took away things that

    I could have sworn

        were right there.

Now I know

  they're still there.

Darkness can only take

    the shape of things.

4.6.9.38.53.56.57.**58**.62

Sometimes I walk nowhere

    and I accidentally strive

and sometimes

    I'm walking somewhere

  and I

stroll and steal

    some time.

4.18.23.**58**.62

A house is not your home

until you've dropped a glass

   or killed a spider or scuffed a wall

    or changed a lightbulb

and changed the smoke detector batteries,

then slowly

   and suddenly it's yours.

Chapter VII
54,2,51,39,36

Poems about Mental Illness and Pain

and some about Hope,

Emotion, and Sorrow

2.7.13.39.51.53.**54**

Depression is weird

   cause sometimes

days of shit

     go by

and then I realize,

"wait a second

  I'm a positive

     person!!"

and it replies

"Oh, right,

  yeah, sorry."

6.15.53.**54**.56

I didn't lose my mind,

I know exactly where I

     left it.

2.**54**

I already

  got that kind of help,

It didn't help.

    .

2.33.49.**54**

"That's a crutch," they said.

"Yeah,

    can't you see I'm fucking limping?"

2.6.12.15.31.37.53.**54**.58

I'm writing in my head

    but none of it is saved

so if you can read my mind

    please,

    remember what it says.

12.15.36.37.39.42.43.53.**54**

I do not hear voices.

I do, however

   have rough drafts

of every

    conversation

and altercation

     my brain thinks

might possibly happen,

with no eraser in sight.

2.20.46.48.**54**

There's a schizophrenic

   in a padded room

  and

   everything he says is true

but

   those doctors that he's talking to

are not

    real to me and you.

2.13.20.22.33.36.41.46.53.**54**.58.61

They took me

     to Hell

  and gave me a tour,

they said, "listen, kid,

    this could all be yours"

I screamed out, "NO!"

    They said,

        "well, now you've been warned"

and then I woke up in

    a psych ward.

7.31.37.53.**54**

Talking to yourself

    is normal,

conversing

    is special,

arguing

    is nuts.

2.33.34.**54**.58

Logically alive because,

no matter how bad

       I get,

I do not know what death is like at all

  so,

it is possible it is worse than life

and then I think

      it could definitely be worse than life

because life is

     at times

   amazing and exhilarating

and

 bad

but no matter how bad

  I get...

2.33.39.**54**

Depression

  is like

  when you have the flu

with nothing to do

  but sit there

 resigned

 to the

lowest

feeling

waiting for

  worse

   better

    and nothing.

2.31.37.53.**54**

I thought myself

   sick.

1.2.8.17.45.53.**54**.56.62

Nowhere near

   as happy as I could be,

but

   now that I know it's up to me,

    soon enough

I will be.

2.34.**54**

Decide to die

       now,

or live

  to not know

    when

   or why

or how.

2.15.37.41.53.**54**

The difficulty I have

   practicing mindfulness

is that I wasn't

      mindful for so long,

I was using my mind like a rollercoaster

         dumpster

    camera

and now it's upside down, smells like shit and

     remembers all the

       wrong things.

2.14.49.**54**.62

Schizophrenics say they're Jesus

   but we feed them pills

     so they'll never save us.

I'm kidding,

    totally kidding.

     Please take your pills.

2.16.37.**54**

Can a white blood cell

   do anything for

     a

   sick

brain cell?

2.13.37.53.**54**

We silently wage

   an unconscious, subconscious war

against madness.

49.53.**54**.62

It's not like I talk out loud

     to myself.

   I'm polite,

     I whisper.

17.47.53.**54**.62

 Exercise, therapy,

meditation and medication

     work wonders

          for me.

2.13.34.37.**54**

I didn't want to shoot myself in the head,

  I wanted

     to shoot myself in the

thoughts.

2.4.23.53.58

Sometimes

     you have to let

the pain

go away.

2.11.13.20.36.39.58.61

You think the hunger is bad

on this desert island?

Just wait until the thirst,

but thirst is nothing

compared to the wind

that just blows and beats you down.

Then the rainstorms come

and soak you through your bones,

when finally the sun comes out

but it just burns all of your skin,

So you pray it will just go away,

but then at night, you're freezing cold.

None of that will kill me though,

what kills is I'm alone.

2.26.39.47.53

Laugh about

    why

    you want to cry,

it's probably

    hilarious.

2.3.19.33.34.35.36.39.53.62

Hearts ache

    more than any

        muscle,

at least you're

    making gains.

2.6.13

It's painful

    reaching for something

and not grasping,

but

   never reaching

and knowing you

     could have

will hurt

   a lot longer.

2.14.19.32.42

I don't care if you

     don't believe in God

as long as you are kind,

and

I don't care how much

    you pray

if you don't acknowledge other's

     pain.

2.20.31.33.34.36.39.49.62

Live laugh love?

    more like

        cry. hide. die.

2.18

We've all

    got friends,

we'll never

    see again.

2.4.33.35

Adults remember the exact last

    time they cried,

kids cry all the time but can

    kiss it goodbye,

just give mom a hug,

    and smile for the rest of the day.

INTERLUDE SEVEN
On Parents

My parents support me in more ways than I can count or list on paper, but here are a few anyway. When I wanted to drum, they bought me drums; when I wanted to fly, they brought me to an airport; when I needed to go to the hospital, they took me to the hospital and stayed with me until I needed to be alone, and visited me after so I never was alone.

I said I couldn't list them, but there were a few just so you get the general idea. My parents should write a book on parenting that has zero technique but is more like a warning for what you're getting into.

8.18.23.40.47.**51**.56

There is a revolution

      coming,

not a political one

      a political revolution is just a war.

A new revolution.

The industrial revolution

      was part of human evolution,

similar to when we discovered

      agriculture.

This one

      is the same.

13.20.27.**39**.50.62

If you try to put

      fear into someone,

expect to get

    anger back.

2.6.17.**36**.58

I only

  gave

once.

   I'm sorry

I took

  so many times.

9.10.11.15.16.29.37.**51**.56.57

Fear of the unknown

     is foolish,

look at all we know and love!

2.10.38.**39**

The comedown is

    a bitch,

ask an astronaut.

4.8.**51**.62

Hopefully all these things

        add up, fortunately.

4.6.8.9.17.18.37.**51**

We must pay respect

    to that

which we don't know,

in the hope

    one day

        we are blessed to.

39

That feeling

    you can't quite put your finger on

        because

it would break that finger off.

Chapter VIII
20,34

Poems about Perspective and Death

2.18.**20**.33.34.62

Yes, gang shootings

    and school shootings

and war shootouts

    are all different

  but

we keep shooting.

8.10.11.17.**20**.22.35.58

Complicated existence

seems a lot better

       than

simple nothing.

12.**20**.42

Judge a book

   once you've

read it.

17.18.**20**

The best things

  are

 better at being good,

than the worst things

  are

  at being bad.

4.18.**20**.41.57

Someone took

 a submarine

to the Titanic

  once

but it's all alone

  down there now.

6.7.8.**20**.56.57.62

A few steps

  the wrong way

shouldn't stop anyone

  turning

and sprinting

   the right way.

9.11.17.**20**.29

Appreciate every breath

       you take,

while also

  wondering how cool

it would be to swim and

  breathe with

     gills.

7.**20**.40.42

We have two eyes

    one perspective.

Close one eye

  and the whole world

shifts.

What we each see matters

    it can

      move the world.

12.13.**20**.31.58.61

Pen or sword

  pick up yours,

let's prove which is mightier.

I guess

  it really depends how far apart

we start.

4.10.11.**20**

There is only one day

               and it sits

right in the sun's rays.

9.10.**20**

Look straight up

    when you're walking,

see how still we are.

1.7.8.9.15.**20**.37.57

Every kid

    can tell you

half the fun is outside

the

                            lines

9.18.**20**.40.43.62

Any point on the outside of a sphere

     is the center of a circle,

  if you look at it

from one specific angle.

The world is a sphere,

       so, you are the center of the world,

but

  only if you choose to look at it one wrong

   way

your entire life.

4.8.**20**.21.23.41

Many of us live in the past

 because

   that is what happened

but we can live in the present,

     look to the future,

 and

     MAKE THINGS HAPPEN.

1.2.18.**20**.26.36.39

The happiest comedies

    have a little crying

   in the middle

the saddest tragedies

    had a lot of laughing

the whole time.

9.18.**20**

The very first step in knowing,

    is knowing

there is something you don't.

2.11.18.19.**20**.33.36.37.40

Even the best city in the world

  has a slum.

I'm not sure if the jungle

    has one.

20.37.40.43.62

The world is literally

    at our feet

so why do we spend so much time in our heads?

Hear me out,

    what if we considered the earth to be "up"

and "down" to be the sky,

    so our perspective was

flipped upside down?

    That would be weird.

7.**20**.42

Our perspective is our greatest gift,

    it makes us who we are

    but

when it leads us into violence

    it becomes

      · our greatest curse.

INTERLUDE EIGHT
Ocean Mind

The images roll like swells on the vast ocean of the mind. Words are the white caps, crashing. The idea is a piece of driftwood caught in the current. That idea drifts in what seems like endless water until it washes finally ashore. Where will it wash up? Will it be a piece of trash on the coast of a city, or will it provide fire and warmth for a castaway?

2.**34**

I'm afraid dying

    feels like

  when

  you

just

forget something

and you

sit there

    feeling

forget.

6.8.9.11.**20**

Places that I've never been

       ten feet

from where I always go.

13.18.**34**.49.53.62

I want to die

   with a pen in my hand.

Wait,

    I don't want to die.

 I guess

we do all have to die

    eventually, though.

So, with a pen in my hand!

      No, wait,

          skiing!

Fuck it,

no, I don't want to die.

2.13.20.**34**.40

As one world thrives,

    one world dies.

2.19.20.**34**.42

There was a funeral no one went to

but two men,

   who were the ones who found the deceased,

      where he normally slept

on their garbage route.

17.**34**.35.51

Dying

    means

  you

    lived.

2.18.20.33.**34**

The janitor at my

     Catholic school,

told us

  when we were twelve,

about when he used to be a janitor in a prison.

He had to clean the blood when

       a prisoner tried to leave this world.

   He told us

you slash your wrists down your arm,

            not across

if you really want to

              die

they can't stop

     the blood loss that way.

Chapter IX

47,8

Poems about Solutions and Potential

18.**47**.62

Don't point

    out

every single problem,

without offering

  a single

    solution.

6.8.18.23.42.**47**.51.58.61

We need more

    geniuses and saints,

    to fight

all this ignorance and hate.

4.8.23.**47**.51

Let's be the first

   generation

not to

   fuck it up

      for the next one.

Also,

  I'm more concerned with

    the one 500 years from now

not 50.

3.6.17.19.23.32.40.42.**47**.51

Help the person

       right next to you,

and if they all seem

      okay,

you're in a good position

    to

help the world.

1.3.18.**47**

The secret

  is being

    happy

someone else is happy.

8.19.20.27.42.**47**

If you admit you may be

wrong,

I'll admit you may be

        right,

then we can

    actually

      talk.

8.9.11.19.20.23.40.42.44.**47**.51.56.59

Any of the damage

    humans have done to

this

    beautiful

        Earth

is a great

    opportunity

redeem

       ourselves

and prove how amazing

      we

        are

when we start

    saving

and preserving

    the other

species of this planet.

6.7.8.18.31.37.**47**

The world is divided

optimists against realists

    and

believers against skeptics,

but those optimistic

    skeptics

and the realist

    believers,

will bring this world together

    and save it.

And anyone else coming together,

    for that matter.

4.8.20.31.**47**.56.62

We must think of

    posterity,

or prosperity

    will

    cease.

16.18.27.31.**47**.62

"Who's they?"

wins a lot

    of arguments.

  '

19.20.37.**47**.62

Open mind

   and?!

an open heart?!

Good start!

2.33.36.37.39.**47**

Please tell me

why your brow is furrowed,

   and your gaze is cast down,

or

  at least

    tell another.

1.8.**47**.53.56

To be successful

      at what you want

to do

make it what you

      must do

2.31.39.**47**

When deep breaths

    aren't doing it for you,

try yelling

  "FUCK OFF!"

3.18.19.20.32.42.**47**.62

Focus more on

    morals before your methods,

suddenly

  a lot more of us agree.

8.18.20.23.40.**47**.51

It is not one thing

     that is wrong

with the world,

   and not

one thing

    to fix it,

but if we each do one good thing,

       it will be done in no time.

2.40.**47**.60

Perfect world political view!

You forgive the atrocities

    we committed on you,

we forgive the atrocities

    you committed on us.

Deal?

9.16.18.37.**47**.62

Science is pretty cool

   because it says,

"Hey, let's look into this

  so we're not wrong

about it anymore"

Thanks science!

  I didn't even know.

8.31.40.42.**47**.62

Fix education,

  fix population,

fix the world.

Build a colony on Pluto.

6.7.**8**.11.23.38.56.57

Follow

  the path

    'til

you're the one making it,

    there is always

a way

     forward.

4.6.**8**.11.53.56.57

I have my whole life

    to climb this mountain,

but I also have right now.

INTERLUDE NINE
Heaven Isn't Hell

Is Hell anywhere that isn't Heaven? Or is Heaven anywhere that isn't Hell? Based on their nature, Heaven is everywhere that isn't Hell. Hell is the worst pit of what is possible. Heaven is peace and tranquility.

Sadly Hell is real. Hell exists on Earth in many places and forms. It is in the cold if you are freezing, it is in the hunger if you don't have food. Hell exists. Pain, fear. The unspeakable things we do to one another. Anywhere one might say, "It was Hell on Earth."

So, knowing that Hell exists. If you are not in it; I believe you find yourself in Heaven. This library I'm sitting in, and the grocery store later. Our long conversation. It is all so pure and free and good. That is what I think Heaven is.

So if you know pain, I pray you feel a little better and have a normal, good, possibly average day.

1.7.**8**.17.23.51.53

Sometimes

  I come across

      an

awkward random

    kind of

confidence

    that is exactly what I needed,

and wonder how long

    it has been there

happy to use it.

7.**8**.11.58.61

No one tells a

    tree where to

    put its leaves,

it just stretches

    towards the light

    and breathes.

7.**8**.20.37.42.62

It used to be simple

    you could be

school smart or street smart.

Now, there's internet smart,

  you can

    just buy drugs online,

and book smart at this point

      is probably a lot better

than school smart.

Flunk out and then help build the atom bomb,

    or defend

      the country from cyber-attacks,

or whatever the geniuses do.

6.**8**.31.51.56

Searching is finding

    if you don't quit,

there's treasure

    buried everywhere.

6.7.**8**.35.51

Everybody

    loves a comeback.

So all those

    setbacks are okay.

8.23.56

There's always someone criticizing,

    so

    don't listen, keep doing.

When they're busy finding what exactly to hate,

        you're ten steps ahead

  with more than

    they can think.

4.**8**.20.23.51.56

Usain Bolt

    took baby steps,

Michael Phelps

    doggy paddled.

Never be scared

    to start something.

Chapter X

10,30,48,9

Poems about the Universe and Aliens

and some about Paradox

and Wonder

8.**10**.16.18.58

Are we in a,

  horror,

comedy,

  fantasy,

tragedy,

  romance,

western,

  musical?

Yes

 of course, we are,

we're in a Universe.

10.11.13.20.28.62

Our problems are

  tiny,

two planets just collided up there.

9.**10**.18.20.22.58

At life's

most still,

  asleep

    in the dead

      of night,

we whip across the universe.

  because

the Earth is always flying.

      I guess there's some

      place

    we're all

  supposed to be.

                            •

10.12.15.20.22.30.43.62

Everything we

  consider real

is a science fiction story

someplace we don't

    consider real.

10.16.20.31.40.46.58.62

Wait,

  if space

is also known

    as the heavens

and

    Earth

is floating

      in space

then Earth is floating in Heaven?

4.6.9.**10**.29.58

Look how

    dark

  between these stars

but look

   long enough through Hubble,

      to see

there is only

      light

6.8.**10**.11.23.28.38.42.47.51.56.57.59

The potential in the universe

is absurd.

Every human could have everything

piles of gold, water to piss in, sugar, and protein.

It's out there,

floating.

We just need to overcome

the distance between stars.

4.**10**.17.62

The universe is brave

to

exist every day

10.16.20.38

A billion miles away,

   is it night

       or is it day?

2.8.**10**.18.51.58.61

The universe is so large,

every soul has its own

       star,

but we're greedy over

tiny patches of Earth,

to clothe and feed us

     the universe

       yearns.

10.11.37

The sun feeds our bodies,

    with animals and plants.

The stars feed our thoughts,

    with wonder

        of what else.

2.4.**10**.20.53.54

Been to Hell

    Heaven

and back to Earth

not sure

which I prefer,

still have to check out

    the Universe.

10.11.29.40

The world is

  black and white

and

   purple

and blue

    and

 actually mostly

  blue and green and brown

but space is black

     but stars are

  all colors

  and if you look correctly

stars block out

   all the black.

10.13.16.43

What if

    every black hole is

        a place in the universe

where humans evolved?

I would

    volunteer to jump into

one.

8.**10**.17.20.29

Wow, what a tiny

    window we've been given

to see tiny parts of this universe we're in

    and

Wow! Look at all we do see!

10.11.14

There is a UFO

    that comes every morning

and leaves at night.

      It can burn things

and blind people,

but I swear

    it's millions of miles away

and it gives off a crazy amount of light.

Humans

    tend to forget about it.

9.10.11.29.**30**.35.44

I strongly believe in aliens

    and I really want to see one,

but looking at the weirdest animals

    here on Earth

        will do for now.

Platypus and panda,

    jellyfish and elephants,

giraffes and kangaroos.

    Animals make me believe

in aliens even more.

18.**30**

The aliens haven't come

    down,

cause they hate how

    we smell.

14.**30**.43.46

God didn't want

     me in Heaven

     but

he thought Hell

     was too harsh.

So, he gave me to the aliens.

2.4.8.10.13.15.21.23.28.**30**.43.47.50.51.57

We have two futures

according to my favorite

         fiction.

We have a wasteland

   where we fight each other,

or we have spaceships

where we fight

     aliens.

It's obvious which one

     I want.

6.11.16.**30**.40.62

Most of this world

is water

so, if aliens

    came wouldn't they

talk to the fish first?

And wait,

     rocks and trees

and earthlings too!

So, who are the aliens talking to?

This seems like a problem

     our best minds should be on.

6.10.20.**30**.62

Our body is a spaceship

     our mind is mission control

our soul is the passenger

and all the other stuff floating around

       are

        the aliens.

6.8.9.10.13.14.16.20.**30**.37.43

We are limited knowledge beings

　　　speculating on

　　　　the concept of

unlimited knowledge beings

　　who

may have put a limit on

　　knowledge for

　　　　a reason.

1.3.9.10.**30**.40.47.51.58.62

I want to go up with you

　when

　　the aliens come

and take us up

　　　to

　　　a

　　brand

　　　new

　　　　sun.

2.4.20.28.34.36.40.**48**.59

The atrocities of war

    should only be loosed on mankind

to stop

    the worst atrocities of mankind

in which case it should

    inevitably cancel itself out.

INTERLUDE TEN
Thanks Water

I wonder what water thinks after all we do to it. We make it run our electricity, and we poop in it. There's an island of trash in the ocean. We have fountains and water parks. Water just gives back, "here's a clean spring on this mountain," says water. "Here's some rain for those trees that provide your oxygen," says water.

Thanks water.

7.18.20.28.42.**48**.62

No one is perfect

   but plenty are

      the worst.

2.6.9.17.18.20.37.39.**48**

People hate to

   be told they are wrong

but learning you're wrong

      is so

         liberating.

16.20.**48**

What does the man

   who knows everything

think about

   paradoxes?

      He's not sure.

9.16.31.43.62

Science seems

super obsessed with

theories.

I wonder

  what scientists think

    of conspiracy theories.

Anyone have a scientist I could borrow?

9.15.16.20

What we don't know

              is the majority.

Which makes that little amount

              that we know

that much more amazing.

6.7.**9**.16.45.53.54.58

What am I?

>I asked my brother

>>He said, my brother.

>I asked my father

>>He said, my son.

>>I asked my mother

>>>She said, my baby.

>>I asked my best friend

>>>He said, an asshole.

>What am I?

I asked myself, and I wasn't exactly sure.

>>They told me I was human

>>>when I was born.

2.**9**.18.31.37.39.47.51.53.58

Quiet wonder

>always beats

>the loudest dread.

Chapter XI

37,3,29,32

Poems about Thought and Love

and some about Beauty

and Kindness

18.20.**37**.42.62

Some thoughts

      I would

            like

us both to have.

2.8.11.**37**.53.54.58

There's a weather system

        in my head

it makes planes crash

     and

    forests burn

but sometimes it

   snows

    enough to ski

or

rains enough

   for things to grow.

8.18.**37**.42.62

HUMANS HAVE

    THE BASIC RIGHT TO

KNOWLEDGE

this is becoming more

    important

everyday.

9.15.18.**37**

Good things

    come

        to

those who

        think.

2.**37**

Here's a thought!

        Ah fuck,

                there it goes.

11.15.**37**.53

An open mind

    finds flaws

       in thoughts

and as the brain freeze thaws

    dams break down

and rivers erode

    into brand new canyons

in your neurons.

It only hurts a little.

6.13.20.31.**37**.53

Concentration

    without any mindfulness

is obsession.

8.11.15.19.**37**

Cultivate healthy

thoughts,

human's greatest crop.

15.16.20.**37**.43.53

I was before,

I thought?

6.9.15.31.**37**

Pondering is wandering

the halls of the

mind,

poking through

the shelves

dusting

off a

couple thoughts.

7.8.27.**37**.43

In the blue corner,

   the challenger

coming in at three pounds

  and driving humanity

toward what is good in the world

   the Heaaaaart!

And in the red corner,

   the current champion

         of evolution,

coming in at the weight

  of all animal instinct combined

the Miiiiiiiiiiiiiiiind!

15.**37**.40

Good ideas are not your own

        just your head their home

until they're finally

      fulfilled and known.

15.31.36.**37**

If the sound waves I make

  and the black and white marks

        I write

hit your brain

      at the wrong angle,

   I'm sorry for those thoughts.

2.17.**37**.39.53

Please make sure to get my thoughts

      out for a walk,

  once in the morning and once

     before dark.

15.20.**37**.43.47.53.62

I knew when I was ten, to spin

    til I was dizzy,

      it was the best way to think

  straight.

8.13.15.**37**

Ideas rule the world,

some of the best

          are never heard

and for some reason

     a bunch of dumbass ones

             were.

9.**37**.53

Sometimes

     my thoughts wander off

but

   who the hell am I to stop them?

It's okay,

     they always come back.

37.43

Not everyone thinks

  why they think things.

  Please,

think why

  you think.

31.**37**.53.54

I hope brains

  burn calories,

mine's racing

      in

      a

  goddamn

marathon.

3.7.8.13.17.23.32.51

Be sure to love

the hapless

      hero

who

    won by

      complete

        accident.

3.6.7.42.51

No matter how abnormal

      you are

there's someone out there

      like you,

hopefully

    they're smokin' hot.

3.4.35.58

We only have a little time

> to journey through,

I want to spend the absolute

> maximum possible with you.

2.**3**.7.9.42

You

> lost some marbles

I got

> a screw loose,

it's crazy

> love.

3.12.13

She was dangerous to the writer

> because

she deserved pages

> and pages and pages.

3.4.19.31.35

Find and love

   someone with a history

find out the history

   of someone you love

and make sure

  love is

a part of your history.

3.13

Love a skier,

     they'll jump off cliffs

for you.

3.4.6.34.35

If reincarnation

     is real,

I want to meet

     you every life.

2.9.11.17.18.20.**29**.51

I know

   the world

isn't all sunshine

    and rainbows

but hey,

        it's got them.

INTERLUDE ELEVEN
Reality Lesson

I have an explanation for reality. Everything exists. Some people think everything exists for a reason, but no. While most events do happen for an oftentimes beautiful reason, everything else just exists. Sure, there are some reasons. Most reasons, however, are stupid.

Here is an example. Imagine a cube, a black metallic cube, with a green button on top. Now, when you push that button, a piece of pepperoni pizza appears in your back pocket. See, look, that exists now. It exists in our brains. It's fuckin stupid, but we all saw it in our brains. That counts.

Just because it is stupid doesn't mean it doesn't exist. It exists, just like everything.

3.11.13.**29**

Her beauty was the natural kind

but remember,

     tornadoes and volcanoes

Saturn and Jupiter

     hurricanes and earthquakes

are all

     natural things.

19.20.**32**

Only talk down

     to someone

if you're telling them

     the route

     up.

11.18.**29**

Sea glass is beautiful

       but we still shouldn't throw

bottles in the ocean.

1.2.11.20.**29**

I bet

  beautiful places

far outnumber

  painful experiences.

Go ahead

      and count,

I'm so sorry

     if I'm wrong.

Chapter XII
18,35,1,45,19

Poems about Truth and Life

    and some about Happiness

        Family and Compassion

1.2.4.17.**18**.39.51.53

ONE GOOD DAY

MAKES UP FOR A SHITTY

MONTH

hang in there.

18.20.27.31.60.62

Blanket statements

keep

ignorant

minds

nice and warm.

3.6.**18**.28.29.39.43

Love at first sight

is just horny,

and I hope you had it

with your partner.

1.6.7.**18**.62

Freedom to eat, speak,

      travel, and sleep

these are things

      all humans need.

We should program this into

      the artificial general intelligence

hopefully, it remembers.

18.20.50.53.62

If you can't

      admit you are wrong,

you'll just be wrong

      more often.

2.**18**.33.43

I walk up to

pairs of shoes

in the middle of the night

    hoping

        it's my sleeping cat.

2.3.6.13.**18**.34.39.49.50.53.59

Women live longer

    than men because

   we keep dying

trying to impress them.

11.**18**.29.43.62

Our middle fingers

    reach

   the farthest.

6.9.**18**.35.37.43

Some learn

      some guess

and some are blessed

        to know.

Lucky them.

4.**18**.47.62

Patience is beautiful

it makes

  hot food cool,

and no one likes a burnt tongue.

13.**18**.24.62

Don't bet against

     the guy

  that spit his gold tooth

in the pot.

16.**18**.62

The first five answers

    work alright on google

but

   the eleven million others

don't know shit.

7.12.**35**

Humans all suffer

   from main character disease,

where tons of shit

    just happens

   to us

constantly.

4.6.8.10.**35**.38.58

A comet travels the universe

   to be seen from

Earth for a second.

A soul travels the universe

   to be seen on

Earth for a life.

4.6.8.11.**35**.47

When there's

   a fork in the river

the current will decide.

4.8.11.20.28.**35**.42.51.53.58.61

Every pebble

      was once a boulder.

I hope our egos

      work the same,

shrinking as we grow older.

4.17.23.**35**.37

Growing is

   process of healing.

Growing old

     is a chance to look back

  thankful for your

health.

2.23.**35**.44.56

Life is only

      heavy

so we grow strong.

4.6.7.8.20.23.**35**.51.56.58.62

Baby step,

    stumble, run and fall,

        run, run a race,

 run a marathon, win a marathon.

Baby step, picture book,

     Mom and Dad read you book,

    you read book, write a book.

Baby step, think of things,

    ask a question, keep annoying,

    ask in school, ask in college, ask at NASA,

 step on moon.

6.8.23.**35**.38.53.56.57

Not everything's an adventure,

    but if you at least venture

something

    might be

        added to your life.

4.8.10.11.23.30.**35**.51

If a planet can sustain life,

    I would bet good money

it flourishes.

18.**35**.42.62

We are all one,

    not in that

        new age bullshit

        way,

but scientifically

we share

    most of our DNA,

our ancestors are all related.

We are one thing.

8.**35**.56

There's been many

    ups

       and

           downs

but I still have my momentum.

4.17.**35**

I would like to keep track of

    ten thousand days,

and hopefully on day

    nine thousand nine hundred and ninety-nine

I can look back and say,

"damn what a

    good ten thousand."

INTERLUDE TWELVE
Rock Waves

The mountains roll and sway with the centuries. Alone at the tops of peaks and bottoms of valleys, but together in a range across continents. These ranges hold the density of life, creating ecosystems for many forms. From trees to snails and from cliff faces to winding rivers, there are both places and lives sculpted into the landscape.

1.4.**35**.51.58.61

Life should be

fun

because we only get

one,

so as we orbit the

sun

let us sing

smile

and

run.

1.3.4.6.51.42.58.61

You haven't seen

the last of me!

I don't mean that like a villain or

anything,

it's happy!

3.8.19.20.21.32.35.39.44.**45**.51

Loyal brothers,

  honest sisters,

loving mothers,

  strong fathers,

best friends,

   be

as many as can possibly apply to you,

        and live.

1.4.17.35

Hear, hear!

   To the next

ten years!

And the ten after

   and then ten after

      and then ten after that!

1.11.17.20.29.37.39.54

Sometimes I must

stop what I'm thinking in my tracks

  and

    remind

      myself of my own

philosophy

which is extremely

        positive

and I must,

  because

      it is so

        easy

to focus on the negative.

So, stop and look

at a tree,

      happy.

1.20.62

Bliss

    can be missed

when

    you're in it.

1.3.32.42

It's amazing

    how much happiness

we're allowed to have!

2.3.**19**.20.32.47.49

Only judge a person's

    shoes

if they have

    nothing

      keeping their feet

        warm.

Except for Birkenstocks and Crocs.

Chapter XIII

43

What?

30.31.**43**.62

The Secret Service

    doesn't seem great at their job,

they're always standing right in the open.

Unless aliens are real

    and protecting the President

is all a cover,

    in that case, they're pretty

badass.

16.20.29.31.**43**

You're underwater

 but not drowning!?

Yeah, man, it's just drizzling.

43.60.62

Leave

   specific

         books

      in

   random

 waiting

rooms.

Go to the dentist

      and learn

   about the

Blank Spots on the Map.

6.31.**43**.53

I didn't have

      the money

to pay my dues

so I snuck in.

6.7.**43**.49

Hey kids!

   Remember

  to try drugs

so you know they're not for you,

and finish middle school

   at least,

and then just find yourself,

   ya know?

2.3.**43**.49.53

I told her I had

   heart trouble.

She asked who

      had hurt me.

   and I said

No,

   tachycardia.

7.8.**43**.53.62

I don't break the rules,

I just never

    looked them up

so I don't really

    know how it works.

28.31.**43**.49

One hundred percent organic

    Non-GMO

    Grass-fed

    Facebook-caliber

    BULL SHIT

4.8.9.10.11.**43**.50.62

If a butterfly

    fluttering its wings has any

effect at all,

imagine the tidal wave

    humans make

just by pooping.

26.**43**.53

I hate when

even

    I can't tell

if I'm joking

20.**43**.49

Night is just

    some other

dude's

      day.

10.11.16.22.37.**43**

There are so many things

    humans are just randomly okay with,

like how something exponentially

       bigger than us is

    tiny in the distance

or how our bodies just

       quit for a while

    when our sun goes down

leaving us to the

       whims of our baffled brains.

2.34.39.43.47.49.**53**.54

I, Tucker Sullivan

sentence Tucker Sullivan

    to death

for the abuse of Tucker Sullivan

but I, Tucker Sullivan

  overturn this sentence

      for being batshit crazy.

43.49.54

A priest and a psychiatrist

    walk into a bar

they see me sitting alone

  and they turn around and

leave.

2.11.16.**43**.49.54

If someone with social anxiety

     trips in the woods alone

do they look over their shoulder embarrassed?

2.20.**43**.51

When there's something

     in your eye

don't get mad

     it might be an eyelash

 you can make a wish!

If it is not an eyelash

    go ahead and curse,

that shit's annoying.

8.10.**43**.62

Nothing ever

  revolves around you.

It might go

      around once

but that's all your getting.

13.20.**43**.62

Now remember,

    when you're up there

        be careful

  those tight ropes

can be very thin.

"Okay, thanks.. anything else?"

Oh yes, yes

  try not to fall

it's quite a way down.

"Thanks.."

8.13.15.**43**.62

Sure! You can do weird medical tests on me!

Everyone knows,

    bad science

        makes

            superheroes.

6.8.11.23.29.35.**43**.51.56

The cater

    pillars,

so the butter

        can fly.

9.13.20.37.**43**.54.62

Things are bad

    when the schizophrenic

    is being

the realistic one.

INTERLUDE THIRTEEN
Buried

One day

we will bury our guns

with our dead.

30.**43**.62

My hometown

    is known for

the Boston bomber's

        college.

Where I live now is

    known for

an old couple

    that got

      abducted

  by aliens

in the 60s.

That's it, really.

43.49.53.62

Dude's

    dumb enough

to be

    sarcastic on a polygraph.

2.13.19.**43**

Can I get a ride to

     the hospital?

I got gas money.

13.42.**43**.47.62

Humans are weird,

    for example

 we had to invent

      smaller boats

to put inside our boats

    so if our boats

  sank

we would still have

    a

 boat.

And when we die,

    we take the good parts out

and reuse them.

16.18.37.**43**.53

Do you ever

    whisper to

  yourself

"yeah, good point"

15.16.37.**43**.53.62

I have a bunch of made-up theories

  that

I don't know if I even believe in myself

  but

they remain

    in my head

or on some page.

Legend of Content

Use this as a guide. Each poem is marked accordingly based on what it relates to. Make number 5 whatever you want and put it wherever you want in the book.

1.	Happiness	32.	Kindness
2.	Pain	33.	Sadness
3.	Love	34.	Death
4.	Time	35.	Life
5.		36.	Sorrow
6.	Seeking	37.	Thought
7.	Individualism	38.	Travel
8.	Potential	39.	Emotion
9.	Wonder	40.	World
10.	Universe	41.	Memories
11.	Nature	42.	People
12.	Writing/Reading	43.	What?
13.	Danger	44.	Faith
14.	God	45.	Family
15.	Imagination	46.	Heaven/Hell
16.	Questions	47.	Solutions
17.	Gratitude	48.	Paradox
18.	Truth	49.	(Attempted) Humor
19.	Compassion	50.	Cause/Effect
20.	Perspective	51.	Hope
21.	Dreams (Goals)	52.	Devil
22.	Dreams (Sleep)	53.	Self
23.	Progress	54.	Mental Illness
24.	Money	55.	Media/TV/Movies
25.	Music	56.	Strive
26.	Humor	57.	Exploration
27.	Disagreement	58.	Poetry-ass Poetry
28.	Opinion	59.	Controversial
29.	Beauty	60.	Government (Fuck)
30.	Aliens	61.	Rhyming!
31.	Words/Language	62.	Just Saying

Epilogue
An American Cruise Ship

A cruise ship is leaving the shores of the United States of America. Those boarding the ship have saved their hard-earned dollars over many months looking forward to their vacation. There is a storm in the forecast but the weather on the coast is beautiful. The ship is large and safe and has every amenity that a person could want. Even if it rains, everyone knows they will have a good experience, and they all deserve time off from their jobs.

A group of Americans going on a cruise is a miscellaneous and diverse bunch. The passengers are from all over the country. They are from cities, suburbs, and sticks. They cheer for rival sports teams, watch different TV shows, listen to different music, and have different values. They are different skin colors, different religions, earn different incomes, and have different opinions. Where they are all the same, however, is that every one of them wants to go on this cruise. They all want to relax, cut loose, and do absolutely nothing together. They all board the ship.

Two of these Americans think they are far more different from each other than they really are. They are the ones who are politically different. These two have ideologies and they are quite sure of them. These are what we call Left and Right, Democrat and Republican, Blue and Red, Donkeys and Elephants.

The two people are quite similar in their feelings toward the other side. They have become sure that the other side is what is wrong with the country.

The other people on the ship are used to these disagreements. It is America, and we can all disagree. It is actually one of our favorite hobbies. We converse and disagree at the bar, at church, or in school. We talk with our family at Thanksgiving and disagree, then we eat turkey. Sadly, the two whose ideologies are so starkly opposed are beginning to hate each other more and more. They are forgetting what they have in common. They are conversing less and less.

The two who boarded the ship bringing their politics with them did so wearing symbols showing their political allegiance. A hat, a shirt, or a button displaying their tribe. They take notice of each other and avoid each other, knowing that otherwise there would be an argument. The rest of the passengers on the ship swim in the pool together, drink at the bar together, and eat at the buffet together.

Then the sky becomes black and the seas become rough. Everyone on the ship is terrified. Everyone gathers their families. The families pray and tell each other they love each other. The ship takes on water. It begins to sink. All the passengers rush to the lifeboats. They put on their life preservers and again they pray.

The two who have begun to hate each other are terrified as well. They both tell their families they love